Spiritual Gangsta

The Search for Truth

By Bailey Chase

Copyright © 2016 by Bailey Chase
Print Edition
Bailey Chase, Inc.

Editing by: Chasity Jenkins-Patrick
Cover Photo by: Shandon Youngclaus
Cover Design by: The Killion Group, Inc.
Illustrations by Brea Blackwelder
Interior Format by: Jacob Hammer

All Rights Are Reserved. No part of this book may be reproduced or transmitted in any form without written permission of the author, except by a reviewer who may quote brief passages for review purposes only.

Dedication

This is for Amy, Waverly, Maggie & Gauge

And all the souls out there looking to connect.

Preface

I wrote this book because I was tired of seeing people suffer from the same common, self-defeating emotions I did battle with for over 20 years. After hitting my head against the wall again and again, I finally started to look within. This is when things started to change for me as I discovered something, a human connection. Before we go further, it's important you know what I mean when I say Spiritual Gangsta. For me, an SG is a person on a spiritual path, one who searches for the truth in all situations. A Spiritual Gangsta, in spite of his or her own fears, will always be drawn to the truth. Yes, we get lost and take detours but we always come back home because it's our fate. Getting lost is part of the process (albeit frustrating if you're attached to your emotions) but my goal is to help get you back on track with a simple meditative tool called witness consciousness.

The book is comprised of three major components: personal stories, lessons learned and how to find your own truth. The lessons are mined from specific stories - mistakes I made, what I learned, and what I would have done differently had my emotions not gotten in the way. The journey begins with a brief introduction from childhood to today. I'll share what I've learned being a professional actor, studying psychology, playing competitive sports, being a parent and witnessing life. Its been an interesting road these past two decades living in LA and New York, with soul searching trips through India and Asia looking for answers I thought would help make sense of it all. While I'm just now comfortably settling into middle age (I have a two-year-old daughter and brand new twins), writing this book sooner would have been premature. Only now do I have the perspective and humility that comes with being a father. In my younger years, I always thought: "Well, when I get there…" but more on that later. For now, let's start with one moment at a time.

Truth

By search for truth, I mean discovering authentic moments, connecting to *that thing* deep inside that resonates in us all – the *human connection*. I'll teach you fundamentals for finding the truth in any situation. It may be hitting a shot in golf where your heart feels like it's stuck in your throat or walking into an audition and you can't remember your first line. It could be a putt to shoot the lowest round of your life or a role that will change your status from aspiring actor to famous movie star, but even if it's not, *the truth* is the same. What I'm talking about is a tangible connection you can *feel* to whatever activity you're doing and once you discover it, you'll want to experience it *again and again.* Actors talk about *being in the moment* while athletes try to get *in the zone*, but whatever the context, the truth is the truth, so put on your make-up lace up your cleats, take a deep breath and let's go.

Growing Up

"A man who views the world at 50 as he did at 20, has wasted 30 years of his life." — Muhammad Ali

My childhood was pretty standard. Parents divorced when I was two amongst rumors of Dad's infidelity, although my brother and I could never get a straight answer from either of them. It was always "he said, she said," so we never knew what to believe. The truth was somewhere in between. I do remember focusing my attention when my grandmother would talk about Mom and Dad and the way they were with each other when they were still together. From a young age, I was already playing detective, on a mission to find the truth. I love my Dad innately like any son should, but I realized at a young age he wasn't perfect. For starters, he's always distracted, pre-occupied, thinking about what's next. He's not in the moment but the positive is we love each other, and his lack of being present has made me a better father as a result.

My brother and I laugh when we find our Dad sitting in a corner reading a book, newspaper or doing a crossword at family gatherings. We've tried to make sense of it all these years, but the best we can come up with is it's part escapism combined with his need to be productive and get "stuff" done. I laugh when my daughter screams at me when I'm writing a text, email or reading a script. She wants me to be present. She wants my attention and she wants it now! On my good days, I have the maturity to be able to exercise patience and put down my iPad or iPhone to finish it later. On my bad days, I get frustrated because I want to finish what I'm doing and am closed off to the moment.

The key to being a Spiritual Gangsta is having the ability to consciously step outside of the emotion and ask yourself:

"Why am I frustrated?"

"Why is she screaming at me?"

Only once the emotion is removed will you have a clear mind and be able to see the truth of the moment.

At age four, we moved from the suburbs of Chicago to Naples, Florida, a small, sleepy retirement town on the Gulf of Mexico. Our Grandma B was already living down there (for some reason a lot of Chicago transplants relocated to Naples) and Mom had had enough of the cold winters. Her hands were more than full raising two young boys. It was a big change that would greatly shape our lives. Life in South Florida is *different*. It's always hot and humid and we were a stone's throw from the Everglades so it was part-swamp, part-beach. Our house was on a small lake with ducks, snakes and the occasional alligator. We also spent a lot of time going to the beach and in the water swimming, skiing, fishing etc. I remember being entranced by dolphins that would follow us in our boat and I loved building sandcastles, but I also had nightmares of killer gators and sharks thanks to films like Jaws. It was an idyllic setting, but as we got older, that sleepy retirement town proved to be too small.

My brother and I would spend summers and alternate holidays with my dad in Illinois, but it wasn't enough; we needed more of a male role model. We fought, drank and smoked weed, and at age fourteen my brother started a drug rehab circuit that would last into his late 20's. My outlet was sports. I got into fights and experimented with drugs, but I was fortunate to have found a better target for my angst. I was sent off to a prep school in Jacksonville, FL (The Bolles School), because my mother was worried I would fall into the same bad crowd as my brother (she was right).

Bolles was a big change for me not just academically, but they had some pretty tough coaches there as well. I found a home in football and baseball and discovered that I thrived with the discipline that was forced upon me. My coaches challenged me to be better and this is where I had my first *defining moment*. I fought a lot as a kid, but I didn't know why. When I got to Bolles, I made a conscious decision to take action and to change my path. I was given the gift of a second chance, a clean slate to define who I was as a person and create real change in my life. There were still bumps along the way (I was a public school kid thrown into a country club atmosphere), but with every failed test, strikeout or missed tackle, I worked harder. Failure became my fuel, my strength. I became obsessed with getting better. I wanted to be the best.

This willingness to change, the desire to improve and increase my awareness were vital components in becoming a Spiritual Gangsta. The goal of Tantra is to turn every act of life into a spiritual practice. The same could be said for meditation, don't just take time out of your life to meditate, but make meditation part of your life. However, at age 14, I was a long way from knowing any of this, but my faith and belief in what I was doing started me down the path of awakening.

Despite feeling like an outsider with a chip on my shoulder, I eventually found my core group of friends. They were mostly other boarding students (misfits) who had been shipped off because they needed discipline or their parents wanted them to get an American education. The rest were jocks because our staff was incredible for a high school. Our head football and baseball coaches were both living legends. The defensive coordinator came from a pro team, the head swim coach went on to the US Olympics and most of the coaches could have easily been on the collegiate level. My roommate was Chipper Jones of the Atlanta Braves, a future Hall of Famer, and being the competitive kid I was, I compared my talent to his and decided to focus on football over baseball.

I didn't know at the time I was comparing myself to arguably the best baseball player of our generation. We were best friends back then and I would go to his hometown to hunt, fish - and we would **always** go to the batting cage. I remember getting nervous pitching batting practice to him in front of *dozens* of pro scouts before every game. Chipper was a year ahead of me so when he was drafted #1 in 1990, he told me it was my time to be the big man on campus (which is silly, but it seemed important at the time). That following year we had some new guys on the football team including two sophomore running backs who had transferred from an inner-city school. One day I hit one of them so hard in practice, he said he had to bounce it outside, "'cause **Big Boss Man** owned the middle." The nickname stuck and I thought it was pretty cool they looked up to me like that. We had a great team and went undefeated, winning the State Championship with a dramatic fourth quarter comeback led by those two kids. It was a *Friday Night Lights* type of atmosphere, going into these tiny rural towns that had shut down for the "big game against those rich city kids." We were a close group and had each other's backs. Life was simple back then.

I had run the gamut of academics at this point. I went from barely passing in ninth grade to the honor roll my junior and senior years of high school.

I even got an award for the most improved GPA. I did well on my SAT's and was getting recruited for football and baseball. I was kind of in between, size-wise, for football. Ideal for a defensive back, but I loved to hit people so my temperament made for a better linebacker. I wasn't super-fast, but was fast enough. I was voted All-State, but not All-American. I visited Georgia Tech, Wake Forest, North Carolina, Virginia, and Duke. I loved Virginia, but I had friends at UNC, and Duke recruited me the hardest. For the first time in my life, my Dad expressed a strong desire for what he wanted me to do. I listened to him and chose Duke. It's a beautiful campus and I enjoyed going to a smaller school. Most people are surprised to learn undergraduate enrollment is only around 7,000 students. I won't bore you with immature stories of pledging or hazing from the older players, but it was all in good fun. I still had that nagging feeling of being an outsider, but I dealt with it and spent the majority of my time

Spiritual Gangsta

with teammates. Some might call it a pack mentality or safety in numbers, but athletes tend to stick together. We're our own gang in a way, which is comforting, but sometimes we hold each other back by not venturing out, meeting new people or trying new things. I wasn't listening to my inside voice at the time and my spiritual path took a detour.

Near the end of my freshman year I was pledging a fraternity and hanging out with a few other football players, drinking kegs and trying to hit on girls like everybody else. We didn't have frat houses, but sections on the main campus that were divided into "quads." Well, this "wannabe marine" (ROTC – Reserve Officers Training Corps) wrestler guy came into our section starting shit. In the chaos that transpired from physically removing this guy, one of my teammates (and best friend at the time) got hit. Afterwards, my buddy told me what happened and he wanted to go after this guy. In my buzzed state, I was like, "yeah," and we went looking for this dude. Well, when he saw us coming his way, he didn't want to fight anymore and took off. This is what I mean when I said *we hold each other back*. Call it bravado, getting called out or just being a 19-year-old, but things went south pretty quickly. My buddy was one of the fastest guys I've ever seen and caught him first. He tackled him and started throwing punches, and by the time I got there "the fight" was over — but my buddy kept punching. I pulled him off because this dude wasn't fighting back. Something inside me said stop and we took off. The guy was messed up and taken to the school infirmary. An investigation ensued, and of course the guy didn't remember my buddy, but he recognized me from the football media guide. Because of his injuries, the police did an investigation, and despite the fact that I never touched the guy, I was suspended from school for a semester and had to do a ton of community service. I didn't agree with my suspension at the time, but in hindsight, I wasn't totally innocent either. I should have never been there in the first place, and we were lucky the guy wasn't hurt worse. Had I not intervened, who knows what would have happened? Was he wrong for coming onto our turf and talking smack? Of course, but being an SG comes with responsibility, and our moral code demands that we rise above it. This was an important lesson on my path to becoming a Spiritual Gangsta.

College Football: I had a few concussions I can remember. This was before all the protocols they have today. I stayed in games and kept playing (my wife likes to say: that's what happened to you! I married her for her southern humor). It was exciting playing in front of anywhere from 50,000-90,000 people, on national TV, being ranked in the top 20 — a few of us even made the cover of Sports Illustrated. It was an intoxicating, ego-fueled time with pumped up muscles and a cocky exterior, but below the surface there were some issues.

I had two *defining moments* that really stick in my mind from college football. One happened my freshman year when my position coach was harassing me to get bigger. He was this short little guy who liked to scream and I seemed to be his new favorite target. He went as far as to go to the head baseball coach and ask him that I quit baseball (because I was on a football scholarship) so I could lift weights all off-season. So not only did he end my baseball career, but he also assigned his assistant to check on me at training table (a buffet where we had our team meals every day) to make sure I was eating enough fat and drinking pints of whole milk. The guy was obsessed until finally one day another coach came over to me and asked if it was too much. Said he had been watching and thought maybe my coach had crossed the line.

In that moment, I missed a great opportunity

to rise above it all. I had a sinking feeling in my gut as I agreed with him, but I immediately wished I hadn't. These are the type of feelings we need to be conscious of in our training to become a Spiritual Gangsta.

There is a right way to motivate players — like my coaches did in high school — and a wrong way. Obviously, our basketball coach has done a pretty good job at Duke and for Team USA (congrats on another gold medal in Rio). Coach K is a master at motivating his players and creating that *human connection*. I'll never forget the pep talk he gave our football team before the Navy game (he went to Army, so his archrival). His intensity, his fire, his passion to win penetrated my soul. It's a visceral memory even today. This is the type of resonance I'm referring to when I say: *you can feel the truth.*

Coach K is a Spiritual Gangsta.

The other *defining moment* came my senior year. We had a new coaching staff come in the spring semester before and we all got to compete with a clean slate. I had moved to strong safety at this point (to get away from my old coach), but this wasn't my natural position. However, the new defensive scheme had a "Bandit" back, which is a hybrid position that's part-safety, part-linebacker. It was perfect for me and I won the starting job. I busted my ass that off-season, had a great summer camp and beat out the new All-American freshman (who was Mr. Alabama — it was a big deal for Duke to sign him, and an even bigger deal that I outplayed him). I was psyched because I felt I had *finally found my place at Duke*. Plus, I had redshirted and was now thinking I would stay for a fifth year because I had two years of eligibility left. I really loved the new coaching staff and my position, but our defense didn't have a definitive leader. With my newfound confidence, I was looking to take on more responsibility and offer to call the plays. That had been my role in high school and I was about to put myself on the line and go into our Defensive Coordinator's office but in that moment, **I hesitated**. I was at the end of the hallway when I saw him, and he caught me off guard when he yelled out to me that I better hurry up to my team meeting. *I froze like a deer in the headlights.*

That indecision cost me, because the following day after practice the head coach asked to speak to me and we took a seat on a bench by the practice field. He explained why two other players (one coming back from injury, and the other was Mr. Alabama) were going to run with the starting defense the next few practices just so they could get some reps. He emphasized that I *was still the starter*, but he needed to see the other guys get some reps.

My heart sank. I knew what was happening on an instinctual level, but I didn't know how to confront it at the time. This would become a catalyst for my Spiritual Gangsta progression because right after that I changed my schedule so I could graduate on time. My football career was over. I buried the emotion and moved on.

HOLLYWOOD

"Be the change you wish to see in the world." — *Gandhi*

It was the Summer of 1995. After graduation, I backpacked across Europe with a couple of buddies and arrived in LA with my yellow lab, Gauge. I didn't know anybody or how to be an actor, but I had convinced myself this was something I had to try. It was a boyhood dream of mine since coming home from school and watching Clint Eastwood movies all those years. I had always told myself, "When I grow up, I want to be like this guy: strong, silent, honest," all good things a young boy should emulate. I had to give it a shot, and if things didn't work out I could always get a real job. What I didn't know at the time was this set the train in motion and those first few years would provide a tremendous amount of personal growth. I tried a lot of different acting coaches and classes. Some were great and some were not. Almost none of the other aspiring actors I started with twenty years ago, are still doing it today. I've thought a lot about why some people succeed in my business and others don't: looks, talent, hard work, luck? Malcolm Gladwell wrote a great book that studies different formulas for success called *Outliers* where he cites the *10,000-hour rule*. Ultimately, I think it's a matter of *being ready* (having done the work), combined with timing meeting opportunity. I've not gotten jobs because they said I was: too handsome, not handsome enough, too edgy, too old, too young or "too winning" (whatever that means). We're all unique and at the end of the day we just have to accept who we are and play the hand we're dealt. Essentially, *love yourself*, so I focus on my strengths: I prefer to listen versus talk, which is a great trait for an actor. When you're *really listening* to someone you create that *human connection*. You're watching, giving them attention, observing, being present; there's a real exchange of energy. I've found when most people interact, it's the exact opposite. Their attention is inward, fumbling through their thoughts, deciding what to say or not say. A famous actor directed me once. We were having lunch and he said, "Most actors try to look interesting, but what you're doing is much better. You're interest*ed*." It was a really nice compliment.

Normally people don't question their daily routines, but for actors it's different. You have to justify your characters' actions, memorize lines and understand what they mean to you so the things you say and do resonate and look natural. I know different actors have different methods, but for me connecting the thoughts is the most important. If I can connect the thoughts and stay in the moment, the rest is just imagination.

My favorite acting coach called it *Natural Law* and he loved to quote Socrates and Plato. I can hear him now:

"It's a kid's game, play-pretend. The more homework you do, the more you will believe you are that person." — Harry Mastrogeorge

I remember the first time I really experienced this was for a guest spot on JAG. It was a courtroom scene where I was on the stand being questioned by the main guy and after a few takes, I literally forgot where I was and what I was saying. I wasn't watching myself or thinking about my next line, I was completely in the moment. It was late on a Friday (maybe 1am?) and someone came over to me after and told me the lead guy never stayed for the guest stars' coverage, but he stayed for mine. It was a nice compliment. We made that *human connection*.

For those who have experienced the highest level of meditation (Samadhi), it's described as becoming one with everything, a total loss of self. We all have the ability to achieve this, even outside of meditation. The truth is the same whether we experience it through meditation, art, sports or life.

If you're struggling with this concept, **don't panic**. As you've read thus far, my path was littered with insecurity and self-consciousness so I know your pain — we're all in this together. Reprogramming your mind takes some doing, and my biggest obstacle when I started down this path was myself. As an athlete, I was all too familiar with the mantra: *no pain, no gain*. The problem with this concept is that it's too narrow in focus. None of us live in a vacuum, we're part of something much bigger. This "me, me, me" mentality just pumps up our egos and fills us with false confidence. It's like getting a cortisone shot to cover up an injury. You numb the pain and go back out and keep playing, believing that you're winning, but what happens when the drug wears off? You're still hurt and you can't play through this pain because the game has changed. Your old formula for success, *out-working everybody else*, isn't getting the job done because acting and meditation don't work that way. You still do the work, but then you have to *let it all go and just be*. The results may or may not be visible and sometimes it's hard to know if you're even making progress. This is something I really struggled with early in my career, so when I auditioned for *Buffy, the Vampire Slayer*, I had a bit of a chip on my shoulder. I distinctly remember the creator of the show, Joss Whedon of *Avengers* fame, looking at my headshot and flipping it over to my resume on the back. After three or four times of flipping it back and forth, I said: "I don't know what you're looking at, there's not that much on there." And in that moment, Graham Miller was born. You could say the same for my career. I don't know why I said it — I didn't plan on saying it, it just came out — but it was honest, real and strangely funny. All the character traits were who I was as a person. More importantly, I had finally broken the cycle of holding myself back, worrying about what others thought of me and in that moment, I honestly didn't care.

Spiritual Gangsta Rule #1 = get out of your own way.

12-12-12

"Don't complain, not ever, not even to yourself."
— *A lesson I learned in Shambala Meditation*

I titled this chapter after our wedding day. As you will read, Amy and I took quite a path in getting to the altar, and it's no small feat that we are where we are today. For those of you into numerology, the number 12 symbolizes completion and we felt as if we had come full circle. We were married in Aspen, Colorado at T Lazy 7 Ranch, in their meadow just below Maroon Bells. It was a ski wedding, which is different, but Amy knocked it out of the park. Every detail from the flowers down to the swag bags was perfect. Although some guests might remember getting cold with the sun starting to dip behind the mountains, waiting for the wedding party to arrive on snowmobiles and my beautiful bride in a snowcat. Hopefully the majestic scenery and warm spirits helped them forget about the chill in their feet. But let's go back to the beginning…

Amy and I met hiking Runyon Canyon. We were both in our twenties and I was still working out all the time and was prone to having my shirt off. Gauge (my yellow lab) and I used to hike this trail in the Hollywood Hills that "can be a scene" for meeting people, but Amy was the only girl I ever met there (I was shy). She was fresh "off the bus" from North Carolina, and when I came running down a steep hill with a sharp turn back into the canyon, I almost ran into her and Gauge. She was bent down loving on him when I stopped, a little of out of breath. She looked up at me with her sweet face and beautiful blue eyes and said in her southern drawl:

"Is this your *dawg*?" (*My heart skipped a beat as I skipped over her question*)

"Where are you from?"

"North Carolina (*again with that accent, sweetest face and eyes*)."

"I went to school in North Carolina. (*My wheels were turning as I turned on the charm.*) Actually, Gauge is from North Carolina."

As we walked down the hill, she told me parts of her life story. She was a twin, hadn't been in LA very long and was planning on moving home because her sister had just survived a brain hemorrhage and wanted to be closer to her. Amy also liked Duke because the doctors there saved her brother's life when he was a child, so she had a soft spot for my alma mater (most people from North Carolina are

Tarheels). I don't think I offered much of anything about me as I was too busy asking about her. She was hiking with her college roommate and her roommate's boyfriend who were passing through LA but arguing about something, so she broke away to give them some space. Before I knew it, we were at the end of the trail and she needed to find her friend, so I asked Amy for her number (this was 1999 so cell phones were bulky, the kind you kept in your car if you even had one at all). She gave it to me and, of course, I didn't have anything to write with, so I kept repeating it in my head. Meanwhile, she was self-conscious about what she had said, what she was wearing (overalls) and that she had forgotten my name (her roommate's dog was also named Bailey).

Our second date didn't take long. I left a message on her answering machine. Remember the kind where you have to wait for the beep? She called back the next day and we made a date to go to the dog park with Gauge (he was our security blanket). I remember being totally smitten and loved everything about Amy: her laugh, warmth, kindness, and she was pretty easy on the eyes. Just as important, she wasn't caught up in any of the Hollywood nonsense and was very close with her family. Secretly I told myself: I'd found *the one*.

But Amy was in kind of a fragile emotional and psychological state when we met. Everything that had just happened with her sister had shaken her to her core. She was suffering from panic attacks, which affected her mood, sleep and appetite. We were young and strong-willed, but also a bit naïve, so it took us awhile to accept that we couldn't fix this on our own. Eventually, Amy saw a therapist who put her on a low dose of anti-depressants, which compelled me to learn more about anxiety disorders. What basically happens is the brain doesn't produce enough serotonin (they don't know why) and the whole system goes on tilt. This lack of serotonin creates a chemical imbalance in the brain, which causes anxiety because those who suffer from it are no longer in control of their moods and feelings. Imagine being 23, feeling on top of the world, pursuing your dreams in Los Angeles and then all of a sudden your mind and body start to fail you? Panic disorder has this strange stigma attached to it, but it isn't anything to be ashamed of (our initial reaction) — it's a real medical condition that needs real treatment.

Hopefully, by sharing this it will help others, because in the year and a half that it took us to understand what Amy was going through we fell into an unhealthy codependent relationship that wasn't sustainable. We started dating just before the Millennium and we were both going home (Florida and NC). I had plans to meet my college buddies who had rented a party house over in South Beach to bring in 2000. Meanwhile, Amy and I were talking every day and my Mom had coincidentally just bought a cabin on the Georgia/NC border and was headed up there after Christmas. Well, I wasn't that interested in the party scene in Miami, so I opted to drive 15 hours north with Mom, her partner and their cat (I'm allergic to cats, so *I must have really liked this girl*). I'm pretty sure I told her I loved her by the end of this trip, and I'm pretty sure she didn't say it back. I've always been very good about knowing what I want, but I met my match in Amy. After we broke up and got back together a number of times, I realized I had to leave LA to be able to move on. This was when I went to New York for a fresh start, but guess what happened a few months later — Amy moved to New York! She said it was to be with her sisters (which was true, all three of them lived together), but of course it didn't take long for us to find our way back together. I had a nice apartment downtown and Gauge was there so we always stayed at my place and usually hung out with my friends, which later became another point of contention. I didn't understand at the time why we had to make it so hard on each other, but we have such a deep connection, it's hard to separate the emotion sometimes, and I was a long way from mastering my *witness consciousness*.

Jung and Dante

"Confidence is contagious. So is a lack of confidence." —Vince Lombardi

It's funny how certain people whom you've never met can have such a profound impact on your life. Had I not stumbled upon Carl Gustav Jung's theories in Psych 101, who knows what I would have become? Psychology wasn't offered at my high school and I honestly didn't know much about the subject. I had heard of Sigmund Freud, but that was about it. Psych 101 taught me Freudian theories about libido (sex drive) and individuation (what makes us who we are), but I found them limiting while Jung took things a step further, alluding to a connectedness. Freud's rationale seemed more scientific while Jung's theory of a Collective Unconscious opened my mind and challenged me to dig deeper, even as a teenager. Growing up, I'd always felt there was something wrong with me (and felt like an outsider); my Dad left, I fought a lot, Mom was battling her own issues and shipped me off to a boarding school at fourteen. Jungian Psychology helped me understand why I had certain predisposed opinions and emotions (archetypes). It also gave me the freedom to forgive myself (not be too critical), open my mind, use my imagination and explore the possibilities. To think for myself versus other subjects like math, science or history where there was only one correct answer. This not only empowered me to formulate and defend my own opinions, but create my identity as well. Brimming with this newly minted confidence, I started to stand up for myself in the academic arena and not just accept the status quo.

Building a strong foundation is paramount in becoming a Spiritual Gangsta because it gives us the strength to absorb attacks from others and have it only reinforce our own beliefs.

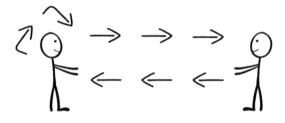

My favorite class at Duke was *Dante's Inferno*. Our professor was this sweet old man, whose kindness has left an imprint on me after all these years. The director David Lynch, who I had the pleasure of working with recently, reminded me of him: a beautiful mind, gentle demeanor and completely selfless. *When you're being guided by someone like this, your walls go down and you become open.*

Looking back on my education, I can see how studying Psychology was the spark of my starting to become conscious while Dante's words set my imagination on fire. I didn't realize at the time how important this was in opening my creative mind (right brain). This awakening laid the foundation for my acting. As I gained more ability to understand others while my imagination took flight: these are my main tools every time I create a character.

I recently saw an interview with Michael Fassbender on *60 Minutes* about playing Steve Jobs, a complicated and offensive character. It was a powerhouse performance and when he was pressed about his acting choices he said: "I only choose things I can play (I agree 100%). You can't play *offensive* (because it's a judgment) but you can play *determined or will stop at nothing to succeed.*"

The connections I've discovered on my path to becoming an SG are universal. You are not alone.

The truth is the truth whether you're an actor, writer, director or you sell cars for a living. Everyone has a story like mine: an insecure college kid who was lost in limbo (Purgatory of life) until his imagination awoke and became his guide. It's not a coincidence that Jung was deeply influenced by Dante and their ideas combined put me on a road less travelled. I decided not to go to Wall Street or right into graduate school like all of my buddies because I was confident about my feeling of a *connection to something bigger, something greater*. I needed to get out, or lost if you will, so I could find my way back home. When we can see these connections *and the reasons behind them*, then we become strong, we become unstoppable because we consciously start living our destiny.

This is the path of a Spiritual Gangsta.

9/11

I left *Buffy, the Vampire Slayer* in 2000, feeling full of myself and expecting to get my own show. Hollywood didn't see it that way and I didn't work for a year. Keep an eye out for entitlement and expectation (it turns people off and can kill your career). When you put out a vibe that you're owed something or "too cool for school," you lose sight of the truth and miss out on making a human connection.

Spiritual Gangsta Rule #2 = be humble and gracious.

Eventually, I got a film called "Killer Rats" with Ron Perlman. As the title would lead you to believe, it's a film about killer rats, and we shot in Bulgaria because it was cheap. It wasn't long after the fall of the Soviet Union and outside of work there wasn't much to do. It felt like we travelled back a few decades in time and all of our drivers were packing guns, which made us question our safety when we hit the town. As a result, we ended up drinking in the hotel bar a lot. I immediately liked Ron and his notorious storytelling. He's one of the only actors I met on a job and have remained close with to this day. As they say in the rap game, he's my mothaf***a.

After we wrapped, Amy and I started talking again, I got a new ride and new agents, life was looking up. I'll never forget the morning of 9/11. She called me around 7am. Groggily I answered the phone and said: "I know it's your birthday, I was going to call you when I woke up." I immediately sat up when I heard the tone of her voice: "Turn on the TV and call me later." She was in tears. We hung up and I turned it on: *pure carnage*. I didn't understand what I was seeing. I was angry, emotional, worried about my friends who worked on Wall Street. I went downstairs to wake up my roommate. I checked on my other roommate, who was supposed to fly back from NY on 9/11 but caught a redeye instead. I woke him up and we all watched in horror. Phone lines were jammed. It was hard to get ahold of anyone. My emotions were on fire. I wanted revenge, and my immediate reaction was to enlist. I was stuck in front of the TV for a few hours, but then I needed to get out. I needed to move around and be alone. I noticed people driving were extremely courteous. It was like time had slowed down and no one was in a rush to do anything. I had an audition, but obviously, nobody went to work that day after the attacks. There was this palpable feeling in the air, like the whole consciousness of the world had shifted. The rest of 2001 was kind of a blur. Amy and I spent the holidays together. What's more important than being with the one you love when it could all end tomorrow? I was up for a cool role in *The Matrix*, but it was right before Christmas and we were going home. I passed on my meeting with the Wachowskis. I wasn't focused on work and was still thinking about enlisting. My insides were raging and my inner warrior wanted revenge.

New York City

"In the midst of chaos, keep stillness inside of you."
—*Deepak Chopra*

The first few months of 2002 were still kind of a blur. I moved to NYC on my 30th birthday. Amy and I had just broken up. I was heartbroken and needed to get away, a fresh start. I was still restless post 9/11 and felt this strong pull to move to the city. I had never heard of Osama Bin Laden or Al Queda before 9/11, but I started educating myself on the politics of the Middle East. I read Thomas Friedman's "From Beirut to Jerusalem" and was on a steady diet of *New York Times* op-eds. My thirst to make sense of it all was insatiable. I learned about Saddam Hussein and the first Gulf War. I wondered why we were in Iraq and not Afghanistan. Was there a connection between 9/11 and the Saudi government? The CIA had supported Bin Laden and the Taliban in their war against the Russians in Afghanistan, but nobody was talking about that. Meanwhile, the whole case being made for war was eating at my conscience. The Bush-Rumsfeld propaganda campaign and Colin Powell's infamous WMD speech left me with more questions than when I had started. I still wanted to fight for my country, but my mind couldn't accept this was a *just* war. I didn't buy what the politicians were saying and my *inside voice just said no.*

Pat Tillman is someone I became deeply fascinated with because if I had an alter ego, he was it. Living a life I had envisioned for myself in many ways: pro football, great teammate, loyal and a deep-thinking dude. He gave up a lucrative NFL contract to fight for his country and stand up for what he believed in. His death was shocking and tragic, and it had a profound impact on me. I wanted to know everything about him and read every book about what happened "over there." I even wrote to his mother to express my gratitude and honor their sacrifice for our country. In so many ways I wanted to be him. Thank you for your service, Pat Tillman. You are not forgotten.

My next job was on *As the World Turns*. I call it my "boot camp" for acting. I learned a lot in a short period of time: how to memorize, multi-camera blocking, communicating with the crew and how to be a professional. A lot of people were depending on me to show up on time and ready to work. I enjoyed the challenge of learning so much dialogue in such a short period of time. I also enjoyed being a soap star in the best city in the world. I dated, went to concerts, games, sat courtside at the Knicks and US

Open, shows on Broadway, nightclubs, you name it. Life got fun again. New York was a great chapter in my life and I'll always feel connected to the city. It gets in your DNA after a while. The blizzards, the cold winters, that feeling where you just can't get warm, the summer heat and humidity, when you sweat through your shirt waiting underground for the subway, the smells, the people, the blackout that found me walking across the Brooklyn Bridge trying to get home opposite the flow of thousands of people trying to *get out of the city*. NYC taught me to tune in to those around me and make that human connection. Space was limited so we all had to share. Living there made me tougher, but it also made me humble. By the time I left, the foundation had been laid. I was ready to become an SG.

Brentwood

"Possession of material riches without inner-peace is like dying of thirst while bathing." — *Yogananda*

Coming back to LA was great. I knew my way around this time, had some money in my pocket and good momentum going forward. Plus, the fact that my new live-in girlfriend happened to be extended family of a big-time celebrity only made our transition easier. They offered us their guesthouse, which was an actual house, across the street from theirs, behind 15ft hedges with a tennis court out back. This is also the very upscale hood where the OJ scandal transpired in the late 90's. We ended up staying for a year.

Our hosts were extremely generous and I have nothing but great things to say about them. Their friends, however, displayed the stereotypical entitled behavior one might expect from very wealthy and famous people. It was a bit surreal having direct access to these folks, and I came up with an idea for a pilot called "Manny's." It was a funny spoof about these celebrity kids being raised by out of work actors and how they would kiss ass to try and get gigs, but at the end of the day it just didn't feel right to expose their friends. Reading the tabloids is one thing, but it's different when it happens in your real life.

Spiritual Gangsta Rule #3 = trust your instincts.

Saving Grace

"In order for us to win, we need ownership." — *Coach K*

Man, I was so happy when I booked this job. *I thought I had made it.* At the time, I was doing this awful telenovela adaptation down in San Diego. Something the network execs had thrown together after they cancelled UPN. **Everyone complained**. They block shot the whole series to save money (meaning we would shoot all the scenes from all the episodes at that location before moving on, which required a ridiculous amount of preparation from every department. We would average a dozen wardrobe changes a day per location and pray that everyone had it all down for continuity). Those who could quit did. I was stuck under contract, but drove back to LA every chance I got. Our female lead (a former Miss Universe) burst into tears when she first arrived and saw our motel. Fortunately, in this case *all shows must come to an end*, and auditions started coming in for my next job, Saving Grace.

Talk about a dream job. It was a hit detective show, set in the south, starring an Oscar-winner with a prime time slot on TNT (the highest rated cable network at the time). My character, Butch Ada, was this ex-football star-turned-detective who rocked cowboy boots and a Stetson (not quite like my boyhood idol Josey Wales, but a good step in that direction). The only problem with Saving Grace was that nobody else could be near the cop Grace was. We were told early on by one of the producers:

Spiritual Gangsta

the show is called Saving <u>Grace</u>. The dig didn't even bother me the first season because I was so focused on watching and learning from my Oscar-winning co-star. I was a team player.

Season Two was different. Relations between departments got strained, ratings were down, writers got fired, directors weren't invited back, even the Executive Producer's tight knit bond began to fray. Everything became stressed and to make matters worse, I stopped deferring to our star as an actor and began voicing my own opinion. This was due, albeit subconsciously at the time, to the fact that the majority of my hard work kept ending up on the cutting room floor. I had invested my heart and soul into this show and our star (who was also an executive producer) was spending more and more time in the editing room. This didn't sit well with the rest of the cast, and the vibe on set became toxic. A co-star detective, who's normally a big teddy bear, was screaming at production assistants on a daily basis.

Towards the end of the season, a script came out that had this weird dream sequence with my partner Bobby and I kissing each other. I read it and was like: *what?* I requested a meeting with the producers and asked them to explain it to me. My character was about to get married but my storyline kept getting pushed back. I wondered if they weren't doing this for shock value? I made it clear to them the scene just didn't feel right to me. The meeting went as one might expect; they promised to look into it and said they would get back to me. Days went by and I became anxious because I had shown them my cards and they did nothing. There were always rewrites on this show, but *that scene* didn't change.

My business can be frustrating at times because nobody seems to do anything until they have to. Part of why I got sucked into the negative emotion surrounding *the show was because I wasn't equipped with a full understanding of **witness consciousness** at the time. I was still taking things personally and didn't have a clear perspective.*

On the day, we had our normal closed set rehearsal (only a small number of people were allowed in per our star's orders). We started saying the words and when we got to the kiss, I stopped and said to the director (who was in our meeting): "I've put a lot of thought into this, and what if you cut the moment before? I'm willing to lean in for the kiss, but Grace wakes up a second before." I believed it was a good compromise, but the director's face turned bright red and then morphed into terror. I looked at our star, who couldn't quite seem to grasp what was happening, and realized instinctively nobody had bothered to tell her. The other producers buried it because nobody wanted to deliver the bad news. As I mentioned before, relations were already strained and that great intensity our star brought to her work could also be very intimidating. It got eerily quiet on set; time slowed down and my heart sped up. The director pulled me aside and asked me to reconsider. When that didn't work, he threatened me with: "You don't want to do this." I felt this surge of strength and power in my body and knew I was ready for this *defining moment*.

This was my initiation to becoming a Spiritual Gangsta. I had already come to terms with accepting any outcome and wasn't going to blink. Our star walked out. The director followed her. The other actors and I sat around for an uncomfortable while and then we were told to go to our trailers. I called my agent, lawyer and manager. They had already been in touch with business affairs from the studio. Another producer, who was a former studio head, ex-football jock and had been someone I looked up to, banged on my trailer door. He tried to bully me with: "You can go back in there and shoot the scene as written right now or you'll be fired, sued and never work in this town again." I drove home.

I felt strangely calm afterward. Seeing these grown men scream at me with their eyes bugging out of their heads made me feel even more justified. Things got worse when they started an email chain with studio and network execs attacking me. I hit right back, which was a mistake. I played checkers when I should have been playing chess. Had I let it all blow ever (*witness consciousness*) that would have been the end of it, but I saw red and punched back. It's easy to see things clearly in hindsight and knowing how the brain works: it gets pumped full of adrenaline and our primal instincts take over (fight or flight, and my ego-filled emotions went to war). Eventually, I met with business affairs and got a nice email of support from the studio head, but I still had to ask myself: was it all worth it?

This catalyst on my path to becoming an SG was a critical lesson because once the emotion subsided, I realized it wasn't just a creative difference but that the producers **tried to force me to do something against my will**. Had they treated me with respect or had I been able to practice witness consciousness, the whole thing could have been avoided.

2008 was a rough year for me. Mom died in April. Gauge died in July. I was in-between relationships and my support system was wiped out. Season Three was uncomfortable. Our star wouldn't talk to me, but at that point I didn't care. I stopped seeking her or anyone else's permission and had become my own man. Grace's storyline was about her personal journey questioning God and why he allowed bad things to happen. Pretty interesting stuff for her and the viewers, but the rest of us were idle. The show got canceled shortly thereafter and we all went our separate ways.

Witness Consciousness

"Adapt what is useful, reject what is useless, and add what is specifically your own." — *Bruce Lee*

This is a concept I was introduced to in my late 20's through a good friend who gave me a book called "Meditations from the Tantras." At the time I was doing a lot of Kung Fu, Kickboxing, Tai Chi and Yoga. I was reading books on self-help, Buddhism and anything else I thought might help get me down the path of enlightenment. I was a Spiritual Gangsta in training! Initially, I struggled with sitting meditation *because I had no idea what I was doing*, but this book really helped me understand the practical benefits of meditation along with the frustration and fears I was encountering. Once I understood *why I was doing it* and applied *conscious practice*, things began to fall into place. All you have to do is witness and observe, aka *let it happen*. There is no judgment, only acceptance and awareness. For beginners, you will more than likely need to crack through your "outer layer" of defenses (gross fears), but in no time you can start to work on more subtle levels by tuning in to yourself and becoming aware of patterns (many of which are destructive).

In addition to becoming more conscious, you'll be able to start using higher brain waves as well (medical research has proven meditators are able to raise their level from beta to alpha and even theta waves in just a few minutes).

This is significant because if you're operating at a higher level (with less interruptions) you're likely to get a better result. So if I feel myself getting pulled into a possible confrontation, I'll rise above it and ask myself:

"Why am I nervous?" or "Why am I upset?"

This not only gets me out of my *reactive mode,* but it gives me the time and space to think, see things clearly and respond as my *true self*. This is *witness consciousness* in action.

Non-attachment

"Golf is deceptively simple and endlessly complicated; it satisfies the soul and frustrates the intellect." — *Arnold Palmer*

What is it I love about golf? I wasn't drawn to it as a kid. I didn't idolize any pro golfers like I did the best players of other sports, but there's something about the pursuit of perfection and the fact that golf gives you *moments of perfection*. Golf seduces you with the idea that it can be that way all the time. It requires a delicate balance of controlling the things you can and *letting the rest happen*. Golf is a lot like life. At its best, it can be blissful spending time with your friends on a beautiful course away from all the noise in life. But then you have a round where you *just can't connect* and you might swear you'll never touch another club again. This is a conundrum that all golfers (and humans) find themselves in. The key is staying positive: *we can control how we react to things*. If I miss an easy putt, I honor that moment, but then tell myself I'll make the next one. By controlling the framing and being mindful, I'm pumping confidence into my brain.

Jason Day, Tiger Woods and the best golfers in the world frequently laugh when they miss a shot, not because they think it's funny, but they know how vital confidence is to their success. If they don't stay positive, you can see their frustration creep in, their body language starts to change and *they're beat*. The important thing to witness is *they're beating themselves*. It's the same in acting. If I have a bad take from trying to do too much or forget a line, I relax and let it happen on the next one. If my two-year-old throws a tantrum, I don't pick her up, I wait for it to pass. The next time you hit a bad shot, forget something or someone screams at you, smile and let go of the emotion. See how that feels. This is *non-attachment*.

For a long time, I was always surprised by stories of professional athletes who had dominated their sport, but had now fallen on hard times. However, when you think about it, it actually makes a lot of sense. Their careers end and many of them have nowhere to go and nothing to do. They're still young and full of life, but have lost a major part of their identity (ego identification). After all the superficial attention goes away, they feel alone, which leads to frustration and depression. It's a vicious cycle that we witness in our fallen sports heroes time and again. Lance Armstrong and Alex Rodriguez are two noteworthy examples because they not only sacrificed their integrity, but compromised their entire sport to win. This is what happens when the ego takes over and people become blinded by their own success. They confuse what they have achieved for who they actually are. The irony is when I hear their names, I don't think: "7 time Tour de France Champion" or "hit 300 in the majors with 600 homeruns," I remember them as *cheaters who lied about it.*

Actors who get nominated for awards go through their own version of this when their faces get plastered on billboards, buses and magazines, but what happens when the media circus is over? When the public stops caring? When your body starts to change in five or ten years? When your friends start doing Botox? You think it will never happen to you, but then it keeps on happening.

Happiness and Meaning

"Trying to find happiness outside yourself is like building a house on quicksand. The work never ends."
— *Pingo*

I really enjoyed reading the Bhagavad Gita, Siddhartha and stories about other saints who set out on their own search for truth because it gave me hope that I wasn't alone. They inspired me to keep going and while searching the world all over, one of my expeditions found me staying at an ashram in India. A friend of a friend had arranged for me to spend time with a young Buddhist Monk who seemed to speak with his eyes. He had this sweet-sounding voice and a gait so free it looked as though he might take flight during our strolls through the village along the Ganges River. We talked a lot about *happiness* and he said: "I choose to be happy." Which kind of threw me. At the time, I didn't realize happiness was a choice (you either were or you weren't). I gave him some of my background and told him my end goal had always been to give back, to get myself to a place to be able to help others. I thought *this would make me happy*. Growing up my Grandma B always told me: "To whom much is given, much is expected." This is seemingly a good thing to say to a youngster, but it caused me to put a lot of pressure on myself. The monk pointed this out and said I would never find happiness as long as I was **trying to get somewhere**. This was one of those moments in life where *everything else just stopped*. There was no noise, there were no thoughts, nothing else was happening, and in that moment his message was clear. He suggested a mantra to help put me in touch with the Universe. To send out a signal for what I wanted, in layman terms: *the law of attraction*.

This was a tricky note for me because up until this point, I had always worked hard for everything I had achieved (ego identification like Lance and A-Rod) and now I was being told I had to *surrender*. For a guy who used to get rewarded for running full speed, putting his head down and hitting guys as hard as he could, was now being told he had to let go. I'll be honest, **the thought of it scared the shit out of me**, but I knew he was right.

A psychic once told me I was a warrior and a monk in past lives. If this is true, it would help explain a lot of my inner conflict. The Way of the Peaceful Warrior by Dan Millman was one of the first books I read on my spiritual journey. The title and story resonated with me because I'm someone who is willing to fight, but would rather get along. At 44, I'm tired of fighting and my heart literally burst open with the birth of my first daughter; now my kids open it more every day. Instead of trying to prove myself and fight my way to the top, it gives me great joy to help and see others succeed in life. It took me a while to understand (*and a lot longer to surrender*), but now that I've come home, my life is full of meaning.

Jimmy V

Jim Valvano was a famous college basketball coach who gave one of the most riveting speeches I've ever seen. He was accepting an award at the ESPY's and spoke passionately for over ten minutes. His body was riddled with fatal tumors yet he remained positive and uplifting:

"Cancer can take away all of my physical abilities. It cannot touch my mind, it cannot touch my heart, and it cannot touch my soul. And those three things are going to carry on forever."

Just thinking about it, my emotions are

overtaken by his and the raw truth with which he spoke created an instant *human connection*. If you speak with a clear mind and open heart, you will connect. I got to play in his charity tournament at Pinehurst a while back, but much more memorable than the golf was Charles Barkley's speech. He was so emotional in talking about the late coach he barely got the words out. There is something extremely powerful and connective in witnessing such a strong man be vulnerable. Chuck was channeling his inner-SG and there wasn't a dry eye in the house.

The Power of Now

Eckart Tolle transformed himself from a psychology student battling depression to a household name with a strong belief in a simple concept. Remember when I talked about success earlier? Timing met opportunity after he did the work and he helped millions of people across the globe. Well, **now** is the time to tap into your inner-SG. Go somewhere private, look at your reflection in a mirror, take a few deep breaths and ask yourself:

Who am I?
What's important?

What do I need to be happy?

You might discover you already have everything you need.

Another one of my expeditions found me trekking through mainland China to find the origination of Kung Fu I was practicing at the time (Wudang). This is no joke, I had actually convinced myself I would further my practice by going there. I had visions of me throwing punches and kicks like something out of a Bruce Lee movie. What I didn't prepare for was that nobody spoke English. I was fine in the big cities but the rural towns were full of poor farmers. Admittedly, I was disappointed not to have found *the secret* that would take my Kung Fu to the next level, but I found humor in the adventure of navigating this beautiful countryside without the benefit of spoken communication. One day really stood out when I got to see this temple that was carved out of the side of a mountain. I remember looking up at it almost in the clouds. The monks there were doing their daily chores, some were chanting, and I imagined things hadn't changed much in the last few hundred years.

Loss

"The Kingdom of God is within you." — *Christ*

Losing my Mom is the hardest thing I've had to endure. A part of me died right along with her. She had a heart attack at 63. It was sudden and caught us all by surprise. I'm happy she didn't have to suffer, but I really missed saying goodbye. That's the hardest thing, the guilt of not being there at the end. The not being able to tell her how much I loved her, the not being able to hug her, to love her back one last time.

I get sad thinking about how much love she

would have showered on my children, holding them in her loving warmth, her laughter.

I remember right after she died, my Dad called me. He was crying, he could barely speak. "It's not fair. Goddamit! It's just not fair…" I got chills down my spine as if time had stopped. All of his walls were down. He was defenseless.

We finally made that *human connection* I had desperately been seeking since my childhood, and I had this epiphany: "Oh my God, Dad gets it! He loved her! He's defending her!" I've never been more proud and in love with my Dad than I was in that moment. Unfortunately, next time we spoke the spell had been broken and he was back to business, asking about inheritance and "Mom's partner."

People deal with grief in different ways. Just have compassion, they all mean well.

Mom came out to me during my sophomore year in college. It was a pretty surreal experience. Being gay wasn't accepted as well at the time. Mom had a lot of unnecessary shame and guilt that she carried around. The thought of it makes me sad. Sometimes, life is too short. She was such a good person and spent most of her time trying to make other people happy, but then her life was over without another word.

My yellow lab Gauge made it to 14. I got him before my senior year at Duke in a small town called Graham, NC. Gauge lived with me in North Carolina, Florida, California and New York. He had really bad arthritis at the end and the prednisone stopped working, so I finally made the appointment to let him go. On our last night together, he didn't have the energy to get up on the couch so I got down on the floor with him. We fell asleep together, and when I woke up in the morning he was gone. I couldn't have scripted his passing any better. I called the vet and they gave me the option to take him to the crematorium or have him picked up. A friend drove while Gauge was on my lap. I sat on the floor in front of the oven in the crematorium and cried, prayed, meditated. It was extremely cathartic, a lot of raw pain and emotion that had been bottled up surrounding Mom's death poured out of me that day. I've never been quite the same.

Gauge was a true champion. He taught me unconditional love through his example of always showing up. Whether it was early or late, if I was mad, happy or sad, even when he was in pain, Gauge would fight through it and make his way to my side. Gauge was a Spiritual Gangsta.

Amy and I didn't get back in touch for a long time after we broke up in NYC. We both moved on and dated other people. I traveled a lot in my free time, searching to find meaning and truth. After having such a genuine, deep-rooted relationship, I was on a mission to find that connection again. While I had fun dating in LA, I didn't experience anything of great substance (sans my ex-girlfriend from NY) and it took the death of my Mother to get Amy and me back in touch. She was extremely supportive and a few months later when Gauge passed is when the channel opened up for me. My walls were down, no more hiding my feelings in attempts at self-preservation. Sometimes we look for reasons not to do things (fear) when we should be looking for why we should. I was open and free to love again. Amy moved from her job in Knoxville and transferred to the LA office and into our little tree house. We got a new puppy named Blue. It was a beautiful time of healing and we had a lot of fun starting our new "family" together.

12-12-12

Blue at 8 weeks.

Branch still photo taken from the set of Longmire.

A still photo from the set of
Batman V Superman

Amy just after our engagement,
wearing Gauge's hoodie.

This is the spot where Amy and I met all those years ago. We decided to go back to open the letter telling us if Waverly was a boy or girl? Blue was very excited.

Victoria Falls.

Our first family photo with the twins.

Me and Waverly.
Words can't begin to describe this bond.

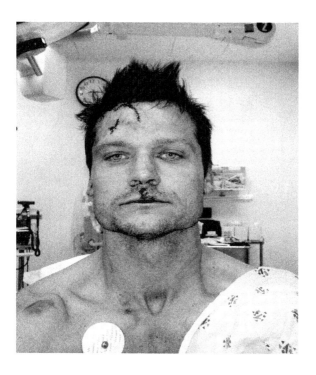

I included this to show that we can bounce back from anything. A week later I was back on set.

A still photo from the set of No Beast So Fierce. This was a drastic departure from any role I had ever played.

Damages

"When you know your deeper mind all pettiness and conflict will cease to be important." — *Anonymous*

After Saving Grace ended there was this weird fallout with my team. I was up for a new show from John Wells, who created ER and launched George Clooney's career among other things. John and I hit it off and I was his choice for one of the lead roles. The show was about a group of doctors who travelled around rural parts of the country and set up free medical clinics for those who couldn't afford healthcare.

As is often the case, it was "decision by committee" for casting the series leads. John got a vote, but so did Warner Brothers and CBS. My team relayed back to me that John was fighting for me, but CBS wanted a bigger "name." This is the same game that happens every pilot season where the networks want the most famous person (so they can sell the show) while the creative people fight for the best actors (to make the show good). The networks normally win, but John is a powerful guy, so we had hope.

While we were waiting for all this to play out, I flew to Vail because I had committed to a charity ski event. Meanwhile, the pilot was scheduled to shoot the following week in Wilmington, NC, so the clock was ticking. I was at a fundraiser and became anxious when my team called so I went outside into the snow. I don't remember the conversation verbatim, but it was bad news: my pilot season was over. I took a deep breath and exhaled. The cold air felt strangely good on my lungs as I watched all of my hard work (and hopes) evaporate.

I flew back home and felt restless. I called an actor buddy and told him what happened (actors like to commiserate with each other). He said, "Why don't you meet with my lawyer? He's a smart guy and reps a lot of A-list talent. He'll know what to do." It sounded like a good idea at the time, even if it was just to vent. The guy invited me to come into his office that afternoon and told me had he been on my team, "You would be shooting with John Wells right now." I left his office feeling better than when I went in. At least I got it off my chest, but as I was waiting at the valet my phone (which had been off) started blowing up.

I wasn't even out of the parking garage when my agent called again:

Agent: "Were you in _____'s office?"

BC: "Yes."

Agent: "Why would you do that?"

BC: "Do what?"

Agent: "Why would you be in _____'s office?"

BC: (this surprised me because how would he know I was in _____'s office?) "Because… I wanted to get some advice."

Agent: "Why didn't you tell me?"

BC: "Why would I tell you I'm meeting with a lawyer?"

He abruptly made up an excuse to get off the phone and told me he would call right back

(which left me hanging…)

Cut to the following afternoon where he was much more composed:

Agent: "I don't want to do this, but we're dropping you."

BC: "Who's dropping me?"

Agent: "All of us: agents, managers and lawyer."

BC: "Why?"

Agent: "Because you met with another lawyer behind our backs."

BC: "I get why my lawyer might be upset, but why are you and the managers upset?"

He stumbled over some words, but there was nothing worth repeating. *It was done.* I trusted my instincts, was humble and gracious and moved on. This became another defining life lesson. You can't give your power away and let others determine your success. I went "all in" on that pilot, got sucked into the emotion and gave my power away in the process. Whatever field you work in, remember: ***You're in control, we all have the power to elevate our thinking and increase our awareness.***

This brings me to *intention and visualization*. They're both important elements and I have two favorite examples. One is from a UFC fighter named Jon Jones, who started signing his autographs "Champion 2011" well before he beat his opponent to become the youngest UFC Champion in 2011. It became a self-fulfilling prophecy but Jon Jones was ready (had done the work), and timing met opportunity. My other favorite is Jim Carrey, obviously a funny and talented actor, who wrote himself a check for ten million dollars and put it in his wallet. He gave himself a few years as the check became weathered from taking it out, imagining it to be real and putting back in his wallet. He continued to work on his craft, stayed humble, believed in himself and was paid ten million dollars for the film Dumb and Dumber. To use his words: "You can't just visualize and go eat a sandwich."

Intention is something, as you're about to read, I had yet to master. After assembling a new team, I got offered Damages, which was going to take me back to New York. I had been a fan of the show and the creators enjoyed my work on Saving Grace so a breakfast meeting was set up near the Fox lot. Everything went well, but for some reason the offer never came in (we later found out they had offered it to someone else).

They eventually worked their way back to me, but I had to leave for NYC in two days. The bigger issue was they didn't have money because they had just moved from F/X to a smaller network and had their budget cut. They wanted to lock me up for two years, but I didn't want to take the pay cut. We ended up agreeing to less money, but I had a "pilot out," which meant if another show came along with money, they had to write me off. I was on a plane the next day.

This is one of those decisions I've questioned in hindsight. I think once I got there and they realized they didn't own me, it made them nervous to write for me. My character had a nice introduction with Rose Byrne that established our relationship (which had already been written), but after that, it was a slow burn. The storylines they had pitched to me back in LA included a major conflict with Glenn Close, but when that never materialized, I began to question why I was commuting cross-country just to say a few lines?

I wish I had been more conscious of my negative attitude at the time.

Meanwhile, pilot season was in full force in LA and there was a lot of interest in me for shows that could take my career to the next level. My ambition started to eat at me. I got close on Homeland, but they went with Damien Lewis (great choice). Hell On Wheels was casting (this is when I was called "too winning"), but there was also this obscure script called Longmire. I loved it. Great writing, extremely visual; the only problem was they wanted someone older for the lead.

I flew back to NYC for another episode of Damages. It was cold, raining, and I really didn't want to be there.

My new agent at the time was this superbly aggressive lady from New Jersey who talked a mile a minute.

"When are you coming back? They want to test you on Longmire. What do you think of the other role?"

I had conflicting emotions about it because I wanted to work and get paid but I also wanted to hold out for my own show. *My focus on money and fame at the time clouded my judgment. I wasn't allowing the positive in and my intentions weren't aligned with my instincts.* Subconsciously I was still harboring negative emotions after getting burned on Saving Grace and didn't want to subject myself to the whims and emotions of another lead. What happened next sealed my fate:

I shot my scenes and was headed back to the hotel when this PA (production assistant) told me there might be a schedule change, but that she will let me know. I told her, "Sorry, but I'm on a flight back to LA. I have to test for a pilot (almost true) and need to get home to my dog (true)." She assured me that it was fine, they'd work it out and she would confirm with me later that night.

I didn't hear from her so I called and left a message. I still didn't hear back, which is abnormal for a PA. They're an actor's conduit to production and are constantly relaying information. That's their job.

I assumed (since I hadn't heard otherwise) they worked it all out and went to bed. I woke up the next day and went downstairs to check out, but the woman told me they had me staying for two more nights.

I responded innocently: "No, I'm flying home today."

I went outside to check on my car service, but there was no car. I was a few minutes early and thought, "No big deal." Ten minutes later… still no car.

One of the perks of being an actor is first class

travel. Nice hotels, door-to-door limo service. They make you feel important (usually).

I called the PA again, but got her voicemail.

I called the car service and they informed me my car had been cancelled.

I called the travel coordinator, who told me the PA (who'd been avoiding my calls) said production needed me for two more days. They'd changed my travel itinerary and nobody bothered to tell me. **WTF???**

I went from my normal relaxed self to so angry I couldn't see straight. Where was my *witness consciousness* when I needed it?

I was out the door within seconds. I hailed a cab and was on my way to JFK in under a minute.

I called my team and told them I was good to

go for Longmire.

This is another great example of what **not to do**. I got emotional and reacted. *Who cares if I was in the right?* The PA was unprofessional, but it was my reputation that took a beating. The long flight home gave me time to reflect on what had just happened. The reality was I'd probably have to go back, and I already felt unsettled about the whole thing.

The next morning, I had a long call with the showrunner of Longmire then hopped on a Vespa I had won in Mark Wahlberg's golf tournament. I was headed to Bikram Yoga to sweat and turn my brain off. It all came to a crashing halt when this kid driving a beat-up Ford Explorer pulled out of an alley around a row of parked cars. He was looking right and turning left so he never saw me coming. My lane was blocked and I had nowhere to go and no time to stop. I laid the bike down and it slid from under me into the side of his driver door.

Meanwhile, I had bounced off the pavement, but strangely popped back up and landed on my feet. My helmet came off when I smacked into the pavement, but I did a quick self-check and the only noticeable damage was some road-rash and torn clothes. I was temporarily relieved until a woman came over and said, "I think you should sit down, your head is bleeding."

I put my hand to my head and it came back dripping blood. Someone called 911. I think I started to go into shock because I couldn't believe this was happening. *I had always been so lucky.*

The paramedics showed up and strapped me to the stretcher so tight I couldn't move. It was all very surreal. If my helmet hadn't had a face guard, everything would have been shattered. Per protocol, they took me to the nearest hospital, which was USC (University of Southern California). For those of you not familiar with Los Angeles, it's in Compton, which is where the LA Riots happened, and is known for its gang violence. It's where they shot *Boyz in the Hood*.

I got rolled into the ER, answered their questions and signed papers, but still couldn't turn my head. I wasn't in pain, just uncomfortable from not being able to move. I heard a guy a few feet to my right moaning in pain, then the sounds of police walkies and their squeaky shoes on the linoleum floor. They were fast approaching and amongst all the squawking, the police started questioning the guy next to me, who was the victim of a drive-by and had multiple gunshot wounds. The cops left and it got eerily quiet.

It was a humbling and vulnerable experience to be injured, unable to move and left alone on a stretcher with nothing but my thoughts. This made me appreciate the fragility of life.

A doctor and intern eventually arrived at my side and told me about my head wound. It's size, shape, that I'd need quite a few stitches and had likely suffered a concussion. I told them I was an actor and asked if they had a plastic surgeon who could administer the stitches. The doctor responded (condescendingly, but she showed so little emotion it was difficult to tell), "USC is a teaching hospital so my intern will be doing the stitches."

I started to object, but she cut me off by saying it would take hours to get a plastic surgeon down here and we should get the wound closed ASAP.

I assessed the situation, and given that the guy next to me was unattended with fresh bullet hole wounds, I conceded.

When I got discharged a few hours later someone brought out my ripped-up helmet and bloody yoga attire and I realized... it could have been *so much worse.*

I asked about transportation and they directed me to a bus stop (this was before Uber).

I went into the men's room and looked in the mirror: *holy shit.*

I got outside and the early afternoon sun felt hot and blinding. I arranged for a ride and checked my messages. There were a bunch from my team so I called them right back and explained what happened.

Team: "Are you okay?"

BC: "Yeah I'm fine."

Team: "Can we close the Longmire deal?"

BC: (Deep breath) "Yeah."

Team: "We're still working on Damages, but

we explained to them what happened and they rescheduled your stuff for next week. Will you go back?"

BC: (My head hurts) "Yeah."

Team: "Okay, we'll close the Longmire deal and update Damages production."

BC: "Thanks."

We hung up.

Standing there, I looked like something out of Mad Max. Bloody, bruised and torn.

I got home and there was a painter finishing up and as I walked in and he noticed my appearance. He apologized. I told him I was okay and he left. I looked in the mirror again and thought: *F- me*. I accepted it, made an ice pack for my face and laid down on the couch. I was thankful to have a week off before I had to go back to NYC. At least the stitches would be out by then. I reenacted the day in my mind and thought about what I could have done differently. I asked myself: "Why did this happen?" The best I could come up with was God wanted me to slow down. I wasn't listening, so he gave me a good smack.

I was supposed to go to a friend's 40th that weekend in Miami. I texted my buddies a picture and told them I couldn't make it. They thought it was a joke and that I was wearing make-up (if only that were true).

I flew back to NYC the following week and quickly realized nobody had told the people at Damages about my accident. The make-up lady called wardrobe and explained the situation. They found a hat for me. It was sort of raining that day and we were shooting outside so it kind of made sense. Word spreads fast on a film set. I ran into

Dylan Baker, who was shooting a scene with John Goodman. He asked to see it so I lifted my hat, he gasped, then apologized.

I met the new director, who surveyed my wound and agreed that the hat should stay on. Meanwhile, the producers were upset nobody told them my head was cracked open. My agents said they didn't know the extent of it, and in fairness, they didn't. The producers did know that I needed to be written off because of Longmire. I was headed to Santa Fe in 3 weeks to shoot the pilot.

I flew home and was in awe of the healing process of the human body. I watched the blood rush around the wounds and swell, then the swelling subsided and I was left with bruises. My face was like a science experiment; it was remarkable to witness.

When I went back to NYC for my final episode of Damages, I was feeling a lot better about my appearance. The swelling was gone and you could barely see the scar with make-up. For some reason, I was on the red-eye and the script wasn't ready before we took off, so I landed having no idea what we were shooting in a few hours.

I got to my dressing room and a few minutes later the showrunner knocked on my door. He handed me my pages and asked to talk for a minute. It was a classy gesture. We hashed it all out and he apologized for how the storyline changed unexpectedly. He explained the challenges of producing the show on a lower budget with the writers in LA (three hours behind), and I already felt bad and regretted letting my emotions get the best of me. He congratulated me on Longmire and we wished each other the best.

I checked out the pages after he left… I had a three-page monologue to memorize in about 45 minutes ("*Uh oh,*" said my inside voice…) The scene actually went well. Good writing is easy to memorize and the writing on that show was always great. It was a break up scene where I listed all the reasons why I was leaving her. The words and delivery were harsh, but Rose hung on every word.

That *human connection* was back and it felt good.

Amy

"Happiness is not something ready-made. It comes from your own actions." — *The Dalai Lama*

As sure as I was that we were going to get married, life had other plans. Somehow, some way our old baggage reared its ugly head and we broke up, *I thought for good.* I moved out and bought a bachelor pad in Hollywood, while she moved into a friend's house. It was all a bit of a shock and our walls went back up as we tried to cope with the damage and move on. The positive is, this turned out to be the final obstacle we had to overcome on our path to getting married. It wasn't until I was faced with the reality of losing Amy for good that I got serious about reprogramming my mind, stopped projecting and consciously started practicing *witness consciousness* in our relationship. I had to get out of my own way.

It wasn't too long after that we "circled" back to each other. Amy moved in and I asked her Dad for Amy's hand in marriage. We got engaged on a beach in Malibu – the same beach where I had spread Gauge's ashes. I'll never forget the image of her wearing the sweatshirt I wore on the last night of Gauge's life. I had kept it in a closet and gave it to her just before my proposal. It's such a beautiful memory, with the setting sun casting a sparkle off her ring, holding champagne, beaming with joy. We celebrated by driving down the coast with Blue and stayed at a nice resort just south of LA overlooking the bluffs out into the Pacific Ocean. While Amy spent the next few months at home working and wedding planning, I went off to Santa Fe to shoot the first season of Longmire.

After getting extremely lucky with the weather for our *outdoor winter wedding*, we dropped our stuff back home and set off on our honeymoon in Africa. While Amy planned the perfect wedding, the honeymoon was all me. I got excited about the challenge and dove into the process, collaborating with several travel agents for every detail.

We started in Cape Town with a hike up Table Mountain to shake off the jet lag. After that we went cage diving near Dyer Island (in the infamous *Shark Alley*. Amy has a huge fascination with Great Whites). Next up was wine country. We arrived at the vineyard on Christmas Day where they had laid out fresh flower petals in a gazebo overlooking their beautiful grounds with baby ducks in a pond surrounded by grazing springbuck. It was like something out of The Sound of Music and felt surreal to be living this dream with Amy after all these years.

The second week we went on safari in Botswana, and the pristine natural beauty of that country and its people is inspiring. The first camp was on an island in the heart of the Okavango Delta where the resident lions have figured out the migrating water buffalo get pinned into a dead end. The lions there were huge and we witnessed a spectacular failed hunt, but it was immediately followed up by a gruesome kill. It definitely made us appreciate life in the wild. Our next stop was Mambo Camp where we saw two rare rhinos on our way in and spent the next few days on game drives surrounded by elephants, hippos, giraffes, hyenas and lions. It was the trip of a lifetime and we couldn't imagine our final destination would have anything better to offer. Plus, we were starting to fade from the wedding and all the travel, but I wanted to stretch our trip through New Year's, and we were so happy we did.

Victoria Falls

We stayed at a resort that had zebras who roamed the grounds just above The Falls on the Zambia side and relaxed on our first night with sunset cocktails watching the "smoke that thunders." It was a terrific mixture of orange, red and yellow rays reflecting off the water floating in the air. The next day we took a guided boat trip out to The Falls and dove in just a few feet from the edge. It sounds crazy *and seemed like it at the time,* but there are these pools of still water that run up to the edge and you can look hundreds of feet down. That afternoon we crossed the border to Zimbabwe and hiked down to the bottom of The Falls. We watched in awe as the "greatest curtain of water in the world" came crashing down and the spray felt like it was washing us clean of the last twelve years of struggle. I've never seen Amy *more free,* which made me feel complete as a man. We flew home the next day and lived in that glow for months.

It's easy to be happy when everything is going well, but the real test is persevering through times of struggle. Amy and I kept coming back to the plate because deep down we knew what we had in each other and never gave up.

Longmire

"Individually we can be good, but collectively we can be champions." — Unknown

I had never been to Santa Fe, but I loved it. It's at high elevation, has epic lightning storms, it can be hot, cold or snowing. It's near Taos, has deep-rooted Native American culture and world-class fly fishing. It's artsy with great restaurants and good tax incentives for film production. It's the anti-LA and was a welcome change for a few months a year. Shooting the pilot was fun. I really liked the cast and producers and loved the director. This would become my extended family for the next few years.

Season 1. It was a long hold period (almost a year) before we went into production on the second episode. Everyone was really excited and ready to get to work, sans one female co-star. She had just done a small studio film and wasn't sure she wanted to do TV anymore. She said she wasn't making enough money, didn't like Santa Fe, the producers had it out for her; the list went on depending on the day. By mid-season I had had enough. It was an early start on a Monday and she had come back from somewhere tired and not knowing her lines. She was literally sucking the energy out of the room.

For those of you not familiar with production, there's a pecking order on the call sheet (which is kind of like a power ranking). However, the people above me weren't saying anything and I was done listening to her complain. I spoke up and said:

"If you don't want to be here, then go. Ask to be written off the show. You're making all of our jobs harder (people who make a lot less) so why don't you just leave?"

It got really quiet on set. Then she erupted, screaming, calling me names etc. Eventually, things calmed down. My favorite director happened to be working that day, and he came in at the perfect moment and said, "Okay, can we get back to work?"

We finished the rehearsal and I went to my trailer per usual. A minute later there was pounding on my door. She was steaming mad, but it was one of the most honest, hard, real conversations I've ever had. I apologized for doing it in front of the crew, but it hadn't been premeditated, it just came out. I had reached my tipping point. A producer showed up and asked:

"Is everything okay?"

We became close after that. She was better, I

had more respect for her and we made fun of the incident in the years that followed. In that moment, we created a *human connection* and put all of our baggage aside.

The show was a hit for A&E. We got picked up for 13 episodes before we wrapped Season 1. We only shot the pilot in 2011 and an additional 9 episodes in 2012 so 13 the following year was going to be a nice raise. We all left Santa Fe in a good mood.

It was another long hiatus, but Season 2 started off with a nice buzz. Two of us in the cast had gotten married, another was engaged. Amy and I were looking to extend our family so it was time to get back to work. The storyline was really strong for me that season as it focused on the election between Branch and the Sheriff. My relationship with Cady was well established and I had a few fun scenes with Henry and The Ferg. The guest cast was strong. The reviews were great. We had solid ratings, but the show still wasn't a breakout hit. It wasn't trending with the younger demo or on social media like Homeland, Game of Thrones, True Blood or Bates Motel (A&E's other show).

The marketing just wasn't there, and as these other shows were getting nominated and collecting awards it began to take a toll on the Longmire family. A&E got squarely behind Bates Motel and gave it a huge publicity campaign, taking it to Comic Con and SXSW in Austin. These conventions are very important when it comes to branding the actors on those shows. As a result, the actors trend and become more famous. With more fame comes more opportunity, more work, better careers and bigger paychecks. Meanwhile, Longmire fell through the cracks.

Creatively, I was enjoying the work as my character started to break down emotionally, He became vulnerable and self-sacrificing, which started a surprising transformation. Season 2 ended on a cliffhanger with my being shot by a mystical Native American warrior. With all the distractions at the network and the lack of publicity, I just focused on what I could control: *doing good work*. Our ratings were still solid, so we all went home expecting to hear positive news soon about a pick-up and negotiating raises. I had faith the Universe would respond.

Well, a few months later, the pick-up happened, but the order was only for 10 episodes and it came in at a seemingly calculated time. The Friday before Christmas, which meant any questions would have to wait three weeks until people were back in the office. Happy Holidays!

*It's funny writing and looking back on this now. The positive is we got a pick-up and I was gainfully employed for another year. However, that was not how I was seeing it at the time. I was focused on what we **weren't** getting. We had a baby on the way and needed* *more income, not less.*

My inner Spiritual Gangsta was being held hostage by my self-induced financial stress.

In January, a meeting was set up with the Longmire Executive Producers. It started out well as we caught up on the holidays, kids, Amy's pregnancy and storylines for next season. I brought up my contract, the short-order (10 episodes, not 13) and the need for a raise so we could move out of our 1BR condo and into a house. They all agreed, complimented my excellent work and told me I deserved a raise, but sadly there was no money for anyone.

My emotions got the best of me.

I went off: "How can you ask us to take a 30% pay cut? We have incredibly long hold periods. We shoot during the busiest time of year (which prohibits us from doing other shows) and you don't pay for our travel or housing because we're considered *local hires*. Why did you agree to only 10 episodes?"

Pregnant pause.

"It's actually better for us to only do 10. It's much more difficult to storyboard for 13."

And there it was. My heart sank as I realized the betrayal. It's like when a player loses confidence in his coach and I wasn't going stay silent like I did that day at Duke next to the practice field. In that moment, I couldn't stomach it:

"I want this to be my last season."

At that point they **had** to write me off the show.

Be careful what you ask for, you just might get it (defining moment).

Being a Spiritual Gangsta doesn't preclude us from making mistakes. Life is a learning process, but our code mandates if you get knocked down, you get right back up.

Fatherhood

"Truth is not something outside to be discovered, it is something inside to be realized." — *Osho*

It's almost surreal to be writing this chapter. I was so afraid of making this commitment for so long because of the disaster of an example shown to me by my parents. They fought for decades and Dad still hasn't moved on. I want to shake him and say: ***let it go!*** But we all have our own path and lessons to learn and who am I to judge? I don't know what his childhood was like, and I don't really know if my mother did something to justify such vehemence. I wasn't there, but for me **fatherhood is amazing**. I'm not big on clichés, but it's truly the best and hardest thing I have ever done.

Waverly came on the scene while I was still working on Longmire. We were in Santa Fe and my wife being the hippie girl she is, Waverly arrived naturally in a birth center. It was such a poetic and beautiful experience (*although intense*). I wouldn't trade those memories for the world. What made it even sweeter was that Amy had been told she was infertile, high-risk (over 35) and we'd already had a miscarriage. So when she was getting close, we were all on high alert. Well, the false contractions came a few days prior and I raced home from set in my cop uniform. I was doubling the limit but figured Branch could talk his way out of a speeding ticket. She was born on May 31 (same day as Clint Eastwood).

The twins were totally unexpected. We were sitting in the OB's office and at this point we'd had a second miscarriage, so I had become adept at reading the reactions of the nurses and doctor. He started laughing… I said, "I think that's good news?" He blurted, "Yeah if you want twins!!" Amy almost cried right there on the table. She's a twin and her mom had two sets of twins, so it wasn't a total shock, but it certainly changed our plan of having *two children*. I was thrilled, but our lives have been chaos since they arrived. Amy and I have days when we look at each other and are like: *we have three children*.

The plan was to deliver them naturally as well, but in a hospital because of the inherent risks with twins (and Maggie was breach). Gauge was sitting head down pretty much the whole time, but as we went from 36, 37 to 38 weeks our doctor started to talk about the what if's:

What if Maggie stays breach? What if you don't dilate? What if… These are real hard questions because as parents, we're literally responsible for their health and well-being. Well, Amy didn't dilate and our doctor said it was too risky to go past her due date and started talking about undue stress on the babies. That's when we threw up our hands and ended up in a last-minute C-section. This was not only a totally different experience, but a major operation. Amy had residual effects for months. I don't know how she does it (primal instincts maybe), but she's a rock star and I'm in awe of her fortitude as a mother.

What's surprised me most about fatherhood is *my willingness to give up on what I want to do*. Every day I find myself letting go of *what I want* and accepting *what is*. Recently, I did an interview and was asked, "What's the best thing about Fatherhood?" It was right after Waverly's second birthday and I distinctly remember watching her on a pony as happy as could be and I thought: there is no place *I would rather be*. That was a pretty cool realization for a guy who has always challenged himself to be better, to keep driving, shooting for the stars, aiming for perfection, to be the best athlete, the best actor, to all of a sudden just let it all go accept what is. We were at a public park and my daughter was on a $3 pony ride. It was truly one of the best days of my life.

When we finally *give up on getting somewhere and accept who we are, happiness will find us.* This is what fatherhood has taught me.

Overcoming Obstacles

"I've never let anyone talk me into not believing in myself." — Muhammad Ali

I'm going to start this chapter with my last job because it's so fresh in my brain. After everything I've been through the last 20 years in Hollywood, I had finally booked my own show. It was called Paranormal and was an interesting story about a washed-up ghost hunter who blamed himself for his wife's death and was unwilling to move on. He was described as being just past his prime and a bit disheveled, but if only he could get his sh*t together… Strangely, I fit this description perfectly, got the offer without having to test and flew to Atlanta to shoot the pilot a few weeks later.

What I didn't know was that the network (in spite of approving me) wanted another actor for the role and if the creator, director and studio knew, they didn't share that news with me. So after the table read, which was broadcast over a video feed that kept dropping, I was recast. This was an extremely difficult pill to swallow because not only had they taken me out of pilot season (which had high stakes for me and my growing family), but I was being sent home in embarrassing fashion. The harsh reality was that I'd probably have to wait a year to get another shot at a new show with a big contract.

It took everything in me not to repeat my past mistakes. I felt hung out to dry and my team hadn't protected me. My body became flooded with emotion but I mastered my *witness consciousness* on this occasion. I rose above my anger and let it all play out: The director fought for me, I had a great heart-to-heart with the showrunner and was told the studio wanted me, but at the end of the day the network has the power. The producers decided they had to give the network their guy or the show wouldn't get on the air. It was just business. Nothing personal. I never heard from anyone at the CW, but I understand the rationale. If you look at their content, I'm not their prototype. I was a risky choice from the beginning and they went with someone safer.

The hardest thing about my business is the unknown. It can be tough coming to terms when things don't go your way and nobody is there to answer to your questions. I know the way of the Spiritual Gangsta is to condition our minds to accept all outcomes, but sometimes the rejection just hurts. Before we can move on we have to deal with these feelings. When you continue to put yourself on the line, things aren't always going to go the way you want them to. It's only human to go to a dark place when we don't get something we really want, but then we need to find our way out.

This is when I remind myself there's a bigger picture I can't always see. Things happen for a reason, just have faith. I wouldn't call myself religious, but I've never found shame in asking for God's help. I prayed a lot when my brother was going through rehab and this is when I first heard the *Serenity Prayer*.

I made a slight variation, which I find empowering:

Control the things you can.

Accept the things you can't.

Be conscious of the difference.

This puts the responsibility on us. Only we have the power to change our thinking (of course, we can ask for God's help), but now *I only focus on the things I want.* Sending out a positive signal that will attract the same. Aligning my intentions with my instincts. I saw a powerful segment from Oprah recently; You Become What You Believe. I know who Oprah is because I live on planet Earth but having not watched the show, I wasn't familiar with her message. As I got deeper and deeper into the lesson, I was like: "Yeah, uh huh, love that." It's the same message an SG sends out and if you do it with a clear mind, open heart and have a strong belief if what you're doing, everything else will take care of itself.

A great example of **control versus acceptance** for me was when I was offered *Chicago, PD*. It was for a recurring guest star and they were only paying scale but I said yes to get back into business with

Dick Wolf and NBC.

After I shot the first episode, I had a few weeks off back in LA and booked a small but coveted role in *Batman v Superman: Dawn of Justice*. I was going from playing a badass DEA agent to a badass special ops dude. I loved that the industry was starting to see me as a tough guy and not just "charming." It seemed like everything was finally falling into place — and *then the phone rang*. It was my agents (*now former*) calling to tell me there was a date conflict. They said I was going to have to drop out of the film. I pushed back because I really wanted to do this movie, had already started rehearsals and didn't want to bail on Warner Brothers:

BC: "Do they really expect me to drop out of *this movie* when they're only paying me scale? Why don't they just write me out? They don't even have me under contract."

Agent: "Well, actually we said yes to them and then said yes to the film. We didn't realize there was a conflict."

BC: "(Startled) Don't you have to get my permission before booking me?"

Agent: "Umm…Yeah, we should have, but we assumed it would all work out."

Life can have a funny sense of humor sometimes, and through no fault of my own, I had two of the largest productions in TV and film mad at *me*. It didn't help when I showed up back in Chicago with a beard I was growing for the film. Ultimately, the schedules did work out, but more damage to my reputation was done. Sometimes bad things happen to good people. Smile and move on…

Batman V Superman

It had always been a dream of mine to work on a big blockbuster movie like this, and the fact that it was one of the largest film productions of all time didn't disappoint. I was only on location for three weeks, but the entire shoot took over nine months. Originally, we were supposed to shoot in Morocco, but there was flooding so we all went to southern New Mexico instead. And when I say southern, I mean the only people we saw outside of production were border patrol. Our hotel was about an hour north in a small railroad town called Lordsburg that time has left in its wake.

I didn't get to meet Zack Snyder (our director) until I got on location, but at this point, I'd already had a couple weeks of riding horses with the stunt guys back in LA and started weapons training with a retired Navy Seal. He also worked with our team on how to take a village, clear rooms, etc. I won't use his name, but this guy was the real deal and once we got to know each other he opened up a bit. I had a lot of questions for him. A friend of mine was developing a show about Seal Team Six for HBO, plus I had read No Easy Day and seen the 60 Minutes piece that described the mission to take out Bin Laden. You could tell just by watching him that he had this motor, *this dude was ready to go, anytime, anywhere.* I was happy to have him on my team and we enjoyed killing time together watching the tumbleweeds blow by.

It was such a huge production there were two caterers (one local and one that travelled). If you weren't on set, you ate with the local caterer in the dining hall. If you were on set, you got a boxed lunch from the other. There were always dozens of people waiting to be called to set because nobody knew what we would shoot next. There were helicopters, pilots, horses, camels, goats, chickens, animal wranglers, stunt guys and actors on standby. The village had been torched with pyrotechnics. The set looked like the apocalypse just happened. It was the most authentic set I've ever stepped foot on. I felt *transported to that world*. People ask me a lot, "What's the difference between TV and film?" That's the difference.

The "How To"

As we transition into the last phase of this book, I hope you've enjoyed my journey but also learned from my mistakes. Even though I handled every situation with honesty and integrity, my ego and emotions have gotten in the way. As a result, I have yet to work for TNT, A&E or CBS again. That said, I just started shooting 24: Legacy for Fox, playing a badass government agent. It's a big-time show with a ton of action — which is new for me — so maybe everything for a reason, right? My path has had a lot of hurdles, but now I recognize they were all necessary. The key for me moving forward is to be mindful of everything I've discussed in this book. I need to *walk the walk*, as they say, and will continue to work hard to create compelling characters for you to watch, but I want to ask for something in return. I want you to report back to me with your progress (or obstacles). We can help each other down this path and make a difference one person at a time. So let's get on with the "**how to**."

Witness Consciousness

Separate your emotion from the experience.

Tell yourself:

> I am not this job.
>
> I am not this audition.
>
> I am not this game.
>
> I am not this relationship.

If you find yourself getting angry or nervous, rise above the emotion and ask yourself, "Why?"

If you find someone verbally attacking you or getting in your physical space, **do not react**. Rise above the emotion and figure it out. You will start to see patterns that repeat themselves. Only once you remove the emotion can you respond as your true self.

Spiritual Gangsta

Listen. You'll be surprised how much you can learn from watching and listening.

Do not let others define you. **You** define you. Remember when I asked you to stand in front of a mirror?

"Who am I?"

"What do I want?"

"Who do I want to be?"

Do not worry about what other people think of you. It's harder than it sounds.

Meditation and Visualization

The term meditation intimidates a lot of people. They imagine sitting in a lotus pose for hours, having nothing but blissful thoughts and happiness. While that might be available for some, it hasn't been my experience. There are a lot of different types of meditation, many of which are moving. There's walking meditation, tai chi, yoga. Once you connect movement to the breath it becomes meditative by nature. You can feel the vibration and once you grasp it, you can begin to direct that energy at will. Connect to your inner Bruce Lee, **keee-yaah!!**

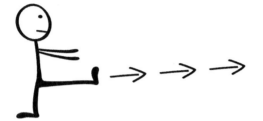

This is the same resonance I hope to have when I'm acting, aka *the human connection*. If I'm in tune with the audience, they can literally *feel what I'm feeling and think what I'm thinking*. There's a real exchange of energy because we're on the same frequency. It doesn't matter if we're in the same physical space (a live play or concert). You can be at home watching on TV and as long as we both have a clear mind and open heart, our souls can connect.

Sports Psychology

My Plan B in my 20's if the "acting thing" didn't work out was sports psychology. It made a lot of sense on paper given my sports background, love of psychology and the fact that I genuinely like helping people. Well, when I booked *Buffy, the Vampire Slayer*, all those grad school applications got thrown in the trash. It was a symbolic gesture at the time, but I can't quite say I've never looked back. While it was the right decision at the time, my mind has maintained a deep fascination with the subject. As a result, I've read a lot of books by accomplished athletes and coaches who talk about connecting to *something bigger*. One of my early favorites was Sacred Hoops by Phil Jackson. I was drawn to it for a few reasons: my Chicago roots, being a Bulls fan and idolizing Michael Jordan. What I didn't know was that the book would bring home a lot of concepts for me by connecting sports to life using the principles of *Zen*. This was a huge discovery because I was still feeling like a bit of an outsider at the time. I didn't belong in the privileged private school atmosphere I had just left and set off on my spiritual journey searching for home. I was new to eastern philosophy, but it resonated within me and now I had Michael Jordan's coach telling me *this is what he does*. It was like a light bulb got turned on.

The truth he was sharing wasn't specific to basketball, but it applied to life. Watching Jordan play, he seemed to exist in a space where time slowed down and instinctively he knew exactly what to do. This made me believe if I lived by the same code, I could fly too. Now I approach life like Jordan would a game, *with a clear mind and an open heart.*

Another coach I like is Pete Carroll, who described his version of *being in the zone* in The Inner Game of Tennis: "It's a mental state that can only be earned. The goal is to be able to clear your mind of all *confusion* and *earn* the ability to play freely."

I love how he places the responsibility on us. Controlling the things we can and letting the rest happen. The best coaches of all these different sports are basically saying the same thing.

Watch pro golfers who visualize every shot before they address the ball. They do it to clear their mind of any doubt and let their swing happen. I took a lesson with Dr. Joe Parent, the author of Zen Golf (who also works with a number of tour players), because I was in my head about some swing changes. His cure was to change my mind, which seemed too simple, but it worked. He told me: you can't *play* golf if you're *thinking* about your swing. Doc and I ended up having a lot in common; a shared love of psychology and compulsive desire to understand people. He invited me to take a workshop, which is where I learned **Walking Meditation**:

It's a deliberate walk. You discover your own natural rhythm. Every step has intention and feedback. All you need to do is focus, concentrate and breathe. It's okay if you become distracted, just re-focus. There is no judgment, only observation. You can walk in a circle, outside in a park, close your eyes and explore your sensations.

Spiritual Gangsta

Martial Arts and Yoga

In the last two decades I've jumped from Karate to Kung Fu, Kickboxing and Tai Chi. While all of them are different and can produce great benefits, I've found Tai Chi to have the most expedient results *for connecting*. It's easy to get started in a basic stance with your feet grounded and your arms hanging freely.

Spiritual Gangsta

Everything is relaxed but supported. You pull the energy up with your breath from the ground through your feet, legs, torso and head. Pause and then release it with your exhale through your arms, hands and feet. Now repeat. You should feel the energy coursing through your body within minutes. If you feel certain areas tingling or buzzing, that is normal and healthy. This is the vibration we want to tune into and will help us prepare our body for seated meditation. Try turning your body from right to left with your feet grounded. Keep it all connected, movement and breath. *Do this for 5 minutes and see how you feel.*

Yoga offers similar benefits. I've tried every variation and they all focus on different aspects of health. Some are more physical, mental or energy-related, but at the end of the day, all of them are just a means to help you **connect**. In today's world of iEverything it's hard to turn our thoughts off and *just be*. If you're struggling with this, focus on your breath: *"Breathe in... breathe out..."*

You can do this in seated meditation as well, or focus on something outside of yourself like a candle, rosary, cross or mantra. Pick something that has meaning to you (Buddha or Jesus), or if you're using a candle (trataka), you want an exposed flame and imagine it in your third eye. This will help with your concentration. *Do this for 5 minutes and see how you feel.*

If you're still struggling, smile and let it go. It's just another obstacle to overcome. Here's one more: lie on your back on the floor (corpse pose). Now tense every muscle in your body and hold that tension for five seconds. Let it go. Just lay there, no judgment, observe. Do it three times and see how you feel... Better? Do it for ten seconds. This is a great beginner exercise for releasing tension in your body and preparing it for deeper meditation.

clenched   relaxed

If you're more advanced you can focus on certain nadis or chakras and use a root lock (moola bandha), but if you're not that's fine too. I'm not a yoga teacher, but I promise if you tune-in and let go, your path will become clear as you gain a stronger connection. Visualize and breathe…

Please visit this page and share your experiences so we can help each other on this path.

Facebook: www.facebook.com/ spiritualGbook

<u>Spiritual Gangsta Mantra</u>

I am not my thoughts.

I am not my feelings.

We're all part of something much bigger, much greater.

I am a Spiritual Gangsta.

Acknowledgements

I would like to thank all of the people mentioned in this book. Without your contribution (positive or negative) I wouldn't be where I am today. Also to all the authors of the books I've read, teachers and role models along the way, your influence was necessary and continues to be appreciated. To all my readers, please be mindful and enjoy the process. Life is like a game. If you want to win, play like Jordan and remember:

Clear Mind + Open Heart = Spiritual Gangsta.

SPIRITUAL GANGSTA
the search for truth

BAILEY CHASE

Glossary

Alpha Waves: the normal electrical activity of the brain when conscious and relaxed with a frequency of 8-13 hertz.

Beta Waves: the normal electrical activity of the brain when conscious and alert with a frequency of 18-25 hertz.

Carl Gustav Jung: (1875-1961) a Swiss psychiatrist and psychotherapist. His central concept was individuation, which is the psychological process of integrating opposites (including conscious and unconscious), while still maintaining their autonomy as a means for human development.

Chakras: energy points in the subtle body that are connected by nadis. There are seven main chakras that emanate from the lower spinal column up through the head.

Coach K: Mike Krzyewski is the head basketball at Duke University. He has led them to five NCAA Championships and coached Team USA to three gold medals at the Summer Olympics (2008, 2012, 2016).

Collective Unconscious: a concept developed by Carl Jung stating that certain instincts and behaviors are inherited (archetypes).

Comic Con: the premiere entertainment industry convention for launching new films and TV shows held annually in San Diego, CA.

Dante: aka Durante degli Alighieri (1265-1321).

He was a poet whose works included the Divine Comedy divided into three parts: Inferno, Purgatorio and Paradiso. The poem describes Dante's journey through Heaven, Hell and Purgatory while alluding to the soul's journey towards God.

Defining Moment: a point at which the essential nature or character of a person is revealed.

Dick Wolf: television producer behind the Law & Order franchises and now Chicago Fire, PD and Med.

Dr. Joe Parent: a sports psychologist who works with professional golfers on mindful awareness and is the author of Zen Golf.

Eckart Tolle: a German-born author of The Power of Now and A New Earth. He's been called "the most popular spiritual author in the US."

Ego: our self-image, not our true self.

Ego Identification: sense of connection to our self-image.

Epiphany: a moment when you suddenly feel that you understand or suddenly become conscious of something important.

Friday Night Lights: a 1990 non-fiction book by H.G. Bissinger, who's story was developed into a film then a tv show about high school football in rural Texas.

Limbo: neither Heaven nor Hell, a place of waiting.

Local Hires: a term used in hiring actors and crew. Productions are able to offset their costs by claiming employees as "local" to qualify for tax credits.

Mr. Alabama: voted the best high school football player in that state.

Nadis: subtle channels in the body through which

energy can flow.

Numerology: a belief in the divine, mystical relationship between a number and coinciding events.

OJ Simpson: a former professional football player and now convicted felon. In 1995, he was acquitted of the murders of his ex-wife and her friend after a lengthy publicized trial.

Outliers: is a non-fiction book by Malcolm Gladwell that examines the factors that contribute to high levels of success.

Pete Carroll: current head coach of the Seattle Seahawks who won Super Bowl XLVIII and back-to-back NCAA Championships at USC (2003, 2004).

Pilot: a television pilot is the first episode of a series which is used to sell the show to a network.

Purgatory: a place of suffering inhabited by the souls of sinners.

Recast: replaced by a different actor.

Recurring Guest Star: a character that appears in a serialized arc but usually has a non-binding contract and is paid scale.

Right Brain: also referred to as the analog brain. It controls three-dimensional sense and creativity while Left Brain controls logical thinking.

Root Lock: (moola bandha) an advanced yoga practice used to seal off the energy from your lower spine and abdomen by contracting the diaphragm muscles.

ROTC: stands for Reserve Officers Training Corps, a group of college-based officer training programs for the US Armed Forces.

Sacred Hoops: a self-help book written by Phil Jackson who coached the Chicago Bulls and LA Lakers winning Eleven NBA Championships.

Scale: the minimum wage a production can legally pay an actor.

Sigmund Freud: (1856-1939) an Austrian neurologist and the founder of psychoanalysis. Freud developed theories on dreams, sex drive (libido) and the model of psychic structure: id, ego and the super-ego. He also formulated the Oedipus Complex and believed the unconscious was based on the theory of repression.

Steve Jobs: the late co-founder, chairman and CEO of Apple.

SXSW: South by Southwest in Austin, TX is a big annual conglomerate of major players in TV, film and interactive media.

Tantra: an ancient science that translates to: a tool (tra) for stretching (tan) - to promote human evolution and liberation. It's commonly misunderstood in the West as having a sexual connotation and has influenced several Eastern Religions.

Telenovela: a serial drama originally produced in Latin America.

10,000 Rule: a principle introduced by Malcolm Gladwell in his book Outliers that states 10,000 hours of deliberate practice are required to master any field.

Theta Waves: electrical activity of the brain with a frequency of 4-8 hertz.

Tipping Point: the point at which a series of small incidents becomes significant enough to cause a larger, more important change.

Trataka: a form of meditation that involves staring

at a single object (usually a candle) to improve concentration.

UPN: United Paramount Network, which was shut down in 2006.

Victoria Falls: aka "the smoke that thunders" is the largest waterfall in the world and has been described as one of the Seven Natural Wonders of the World. It was named in honor of Queen Victoria.

Witness Consciousness: a meditation exercise that allows practitioners the ability to see themselves free from emotion.

Wudang: a style of Kung Fu named after the Wudang Mountains. It encourages a focused mind to control the body.

Zen: a state of focus that incorporates the mind and body. Zen is a way of being.

CPSIA information can be obtained
at www.ICGtesting.com
Printed in the USA
LVOW02s0124180717
541720LV00033B/1568/P